AF425609

MYA'S FIRST DAY OF SCHOOL

Copyright © 2022 by Frances Davis

For information contact:

Banana Leaf Publishing at www.bananaleafpublishingnyc.com or

francesdavis@bananaleafpublishinshingnyc.com

Written by Frances Davis.

ISBN: 9798986557397 (Paperback)

ISBN: 9798986557380 (Hardcover)

Library of commerce catalog in publication date it is available

Printed in the United States of America.

10 9 8 7 6 5 4 3 2 1

First Edition July 2022

Mya's First Day of School

By Frances Davis

Illustrated by: Aadil Khan

"Good morning, Mya!" my mother says, I slowly rise from my bed, wide awake and ready for the big day!

Today is my first day of school! Oh, I hope to make new friends. It's time to get ready. I put on my new socks and shoes. These are my favorite colors too!

My dad makes us breakfast. I'm so hungry! There are fruits and pancakes that taste so yummy!

After breakfast, my family goes for a walk to my school, which is right down the block.

We have finally made it! I'm excited to meet my new friends and teachers. I get to ring the doorbell ready to learn something new!

My teacher says, "Why hello, dear Mya. It's nice to meet you! My name is Miss Julie! Thank you for the apple and for thinking of me!"

I take some pictures with Mom and Dad as they kiss me goodbye. Mom says, "It's such a good memory to have."

Dad says, "Have a great day!"

I follow Miss Julie. Before lessons start, I meet another friend! She says, "Hi! My name is Emily. I really like your shirt."

I say, "Thank you! I'm Mya. I like your shirt too!"

ABC
123
ABCDE
FGHIJKL
MNOPQ
RSTUV
WXYZ

After our morning greet, it is now circle time. Miss Julie gathers the class and says, "Now, we will sing the alphabet."

It's time for classwork! I am sitting with Aden today.
I work on my counting while Aden works on his letters.
Aden says, "Look, B is for blue jay!"

Next is art and crafts time! I play with Ben and Sara. Together, we built a huge rocket!
Using our imaginations, we blast off to outer space, where we can explore the stars!

Off to the playground we go! I am riding a bike with Kai. We pass by Aden, who is on the swing set.

It's a beautiful day with a strong breeze. I join in with my friends and let some kites fly free!

I am catching butterflies with Ben. They fly so high. We let them go and catch them again!

Miss Julie says, "We must wash our hands so we don't spread any germs." I count from one to twenty to make sure I'm all clean.

For lunch everyone sits to eat. We start to dig into our plates. It is delicious. The strawberries are a sweet treat.

It's time for a nap after a round of play and a yummy lunch. Being well-rested is a must.

DOUGH
DOUGH

We drift off to sleep as Miss Julie reads a story. I wonder what my friends will dream about. Maybe it will be the fun we had on our rocket ship.

DOUGH
DOUGH

In the afternoon, we have some time to relax before we end the day. I can hear Aden playing cars with Emily as I draw and color with Sara.

"Mya, it's time to go home!" I hear a voice say.

"Hey, that's my mother's voice!" I pick my bag up and wave to Miss Julie and my new friends. I can't wait to see them again. Today brought so much joy.

"Guess what?" Dad says. "You will be back at school tomorrow." As we walk home, I can't wait to tell my parents about what I did today. From meeting my new friends to learning new things, I must say I had an exciting first day at school!

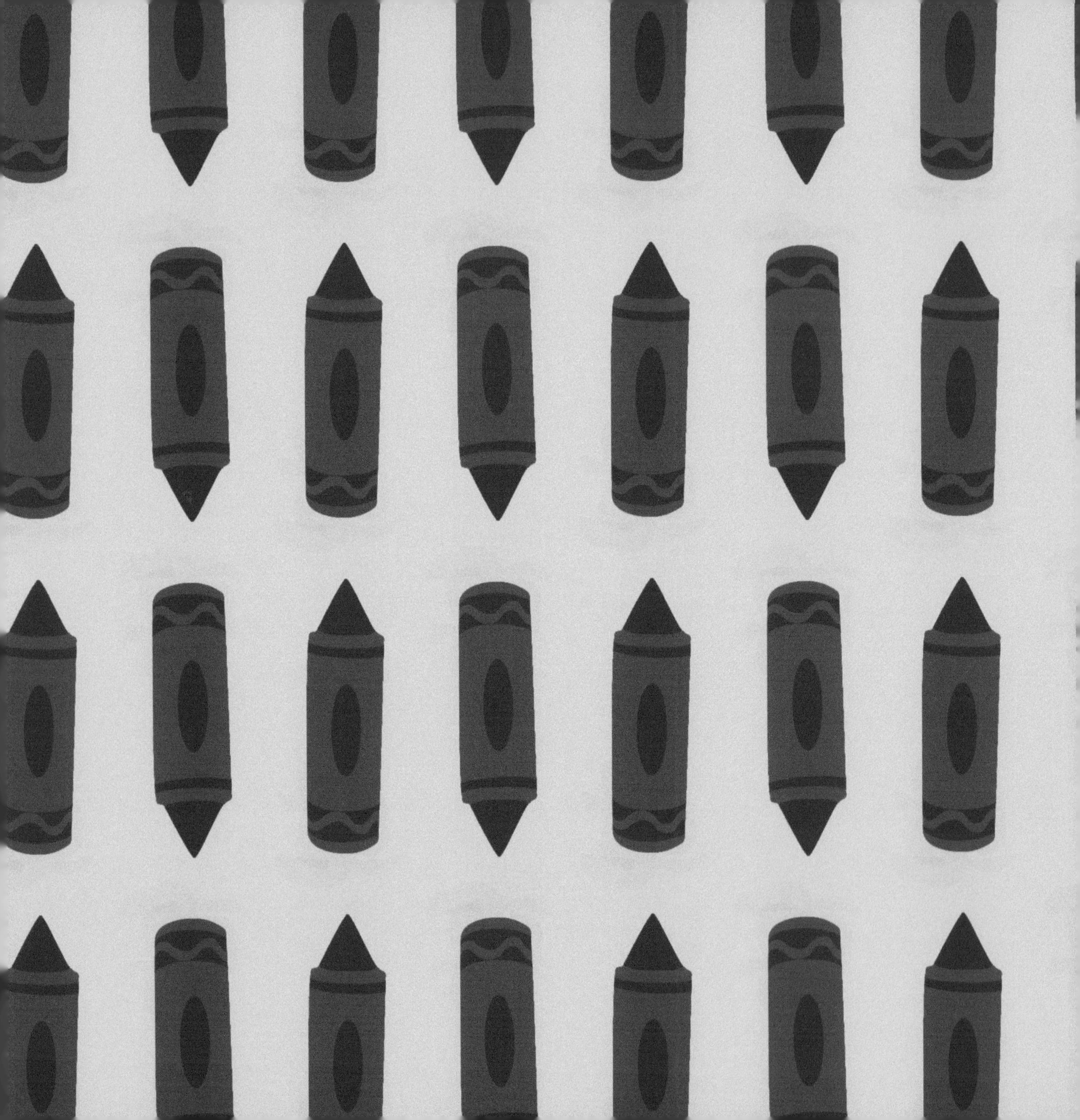